How To Plan Your Career

This book is included in the Chartered Management Institute U.K "Study Resource Centre" and their Library as reference material for both "the Personal Development as a Manager and Leader" and "Career Planning". It is also included in their "Recommended Books" list.

by

Abbas Al-Humaid

Grosvenor House
Publishing Limited

This book is published by
Grosvenor House Publishing Ltd
28-30 High Street, Guildford, Surrey, GU1 3HY.
www.grosvenorhousepublishing.co.uk

A CIP record for this book
is available from the British Library

ISBN 978-1-907211-65-2

Abbas Al-Humaid

One of obvious models of those who applied "Career Planning Methodology" to turn around his life from a small government employee, with serious financial difficulties, and almost no chance for career growth at his 26 age, to become at 37 the first Gulf States national and one of the few thousand around the world, who is authorised by International Council of Management Consulting Institutes (ICMCI) to practice as management consultant.

More than 17 years experience in strategic management, management consultancy and audit in very challenging and senior positions within renowned organisations such as Ernst & Young, Arthur Andersen, KPMG, PKF, Mazars, Government of Ajman (as Group Internal Audit Director and the leader of a total comprehensive change assignment) and Government of Abu-Dhabi (as Financial & Management Advisor to the Chairman).

Successfully established in 2003 a well structured and reputed Management Consultancy and Training organisation in the Gulf. i.e. IMC M.E. (www.imc-middleeast.com).

Developed the company to be the only consulting firm in the Middle East to have been awarded the "Recognized Practice" status by the Institute of Management Consultancy – UK out of 142 practices worldwide. IMC M.E. has also been awarded "Premier Practice" status by the Institute in recognition of the highest standards of professionalism and competence. The "Premier Practice" status has only been awarded to 21 member firms out of a total of 142 member practices by the Institute.

The practice also received the Institute of Business Consulting "The Most Outstanding Centre" Award at a prestigious London ceremony in 2008.

In March, 2007 Abbas has been awarded a "Fellowship" of the Institute of Business Consulting–UK (FIBC). FIBC is the highest level of professional membership, and is awarded to those who can demonstrate evidence of significant contribution to the management consultancy profession.

Certified Management Consultant (CMC)-UK, Certified Public Accountant (CPA)-USA, Certified Financial Consultant (CFC)-Canada, Certified Fraud Examiner (CFE)-USA, Certified Business Manager (CBM)-USA and a member of the Association of Professional Business Managers–USA, possessor of MBA Academic Equivalent- from USA, Postgraduate Diploma in Business Administration from Heriot-Watt University, UK and possessing two bachelor degrees in Accounting and Economics.

TABLE OF CONTENTS

v

Table of Contents

PART TWO
Models and Applications

IMC, Middle East

www.imc-middleeast.com

An International Management Consultancy practice and is the head office of IMC in the Middle East. IMC, M.E. is the only Middle Eastern firm to be recognised by the Institute of Business Consulting, UK, out of 142 practices worldwide.

Has awarded "Premier Practice" status by the institute i.e. recognition for the highest standards of professionalism and competence. The "Premier Practice" status has only been awarded to 21 member firms out of a total of 142 member practices by the Institute.

It has also been awarded the "Approved Centre" status by the Chartered Management Institute (CMI), UK to offer the professional qualifications awarded by them.

IMC, M.E. has been recently awarded "the most outstanding centre of excellence 2008", by the institute of business consultancy UK, as a recognition of its outstanding contribution to the promotion of skills and learning & development.

Book Acknowledgement

Countless people have, often without realizing it, contributed to this book. For that reason I owe thanks to many. The author thought would specially like to express his graduate to Hassan Ahmed Jawad M.D. at Ministry of Health, Oman and Marjorie Gardyne FIBC, MCIPD at IMC Middle East for their dedication to translating, editing, support and whose individual contributions have been particular.

Introduction

The part of our life which is spent in our career is considered the most crucial part of our lives, generally, since it encompasses both directly and indirectly a major part of our time; it consumes more than half of our conscious day, moreover, it weaves its threads to draw the features and details of the rest of our lives and the life of our families, socially, culturally, materialistically, educationally and so forth.

Whether one is an employee with an income that is insufficient for the basic daily life needs, a chief executive of a distinguished multinational company or conglomerate, an owner of a private business or at any position on the career ladder, is a situation that ceases to be inherited in this age of knowledge and globalization, and nor is it restricted to luck. It is you who determines your path in this life!

You can decide how and where you want to be, at which career level or position; you can decide to have your own business; you can reach where you want to reach! In today's world, you do not have to wait for the sky to rain gold, or to find a magic lamp to rub for your dreams and ambitions to come true, all you need is an ambitious, effective and realistic strategy for your life, and the determination to execute your plans!

Thus, it is essential for you to be cautious in planning your professional career as this planning directly affects all other aspects of your life and the lives of your family members!

Your ambitious, realistic and professional planning of your
career helps you towards obtaining success, happiness and
stability in your career, your social life, your family life and in
your life in general, as we say, what is life but a single chain
with correlated rings!

This book serves the purpose of providing you with the
methodology and practical styles you need to plan your career
path professionally and realistically.

In the first part of this book, we will discuss the meaning of
"Career Planning" and its importance, then we will proceed
to explain the "Career Development Model" that highlights
the ideal path for the career development process, which
starts from the individual entering the commercial world
and finishes with reaching the peak of the career pyramid.
Furthermore, we will discuss the importance of "Identification
of the Career Goal". When do we identify it? How do we
identify it and the elements and considerations that affect it?
Finally, we move to a simplified and practical explanation of
the six steps that constitute the "Methodology of Career
Planning" through which you can draw the path and details
of your life towards achieving your desired career goal.

In the second part, we will tackle some general examples of
situations that could apply to you, and we will discuss how to
apply the methodology of career planning to them, aiming at
practically training how to plan your career path.

> With your will and planning, you are the one
> who decides your career and your position in life

Part One

Methodology of Career Planning

1. The Importance of Career Planning

1.1. What is meant by career planning?

The purpose of career planning is to develop an individual's ability to achieve and perform in terms of knowledge, experience, skill and wisdom according to the realistic and practical inputs and the available facilities to achieve the career success the individual seeks in their life.

Your success in performing any job basically requires that you possess certain capabilities and competencies represented in the knowledge, experience and skills necessary for the job role. Additional factors include the availability of correct information in the right time and form, good organizational structure and work environment, the availability of effective teamwork and the necessary amount of generic motivation.

Therefore, when large organizations, in general, begin recruiting, they seek distinguished human resources that are able to achieve, especially given that we are in an age where many organizations have their competitive edge stemming from the capabilities of their employees, management and human power in general.

We are not talking here about the procedures you have to follow to find a suitable job. Rather, we are talking about a path for you to take, through which you aim to improve your capabilities and competencies and thereby enabling you to reach your desired career goal.

This career goal does not necessarily mean you have to be employed in an organization owned by others! However, it does mean, "Whatever you desire to do in life". To succeed in "whatever you desire to do in life" you have to possess the relevant capabilities and competencies. For example, you may wish to run your own business, but to be able to do that and succeed, you have to, in addition to the availability of the other factors, possess the knowledge, skills and expertise necessary to establish the business you want and to run it effectively.

> The purpose of Career Planning is to improve your ability to achieve and perform in terms of knowledge, experience, skill and wisdom to achieve "whatever you desire to do in life"

1.2. Why plan your career?

"Those who walk without vision resemble a person walking off-course. Walking faster only keeps them further away from the goal" is an old quote that says it all.

In other words, a person walking down a path without foresight, clarity and knowledge of the path, without knowing where it is leading them, without knowing where they want to go – this is like someone walking along someone else's path! It's like someone who wishes to go from Europe to Canada, for example, but who decides to take a route through Australia: the more determined they are to get there, the more effort they make to arrive, the further they are from their original aspiration: Canada!

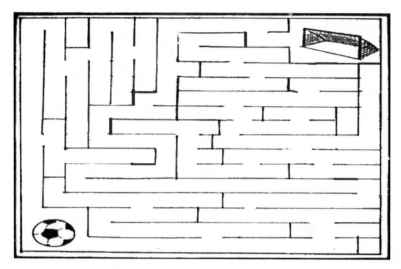

Figure 1 / Maze Game

The matter is really quite akin to a maze game. The net represents the goals you are trying to achieve in life, and the ball's location represents where you are now in your quest to meet these goals. The choices in the game are like the choices we face in life and the different decisions you must make to reach your goals. What happens in real life often happens in this game: we make a choice and pursue it, only to find ourselves in a situation with more choices to make, and so on, until we ultimately hit a dead end, very far removed from our original goals.

In a maze game, it's easy to start over. In real life, though, many years may go by before we discover that we've reached a dead end. At this point you are so exhausted and frustrated that you may not be able to start over, especially if you are not confident that the new path and choice will really lead towards the achievement of your goals.

Despite the great similarity between the maze game and real life, real life is harder and much more complicated. In real life, unfortunately, most of us do not have clear goals to strive for. Further, most of us in real life don't know where we are at present, what we've accomplished and what we should accomplish. Most of us don't know what choices lay before us! Worse, most of us don't make choices as we let life's circumstances take us in directions we don't choose willingly. We are just driven along, usually far from the hopes and dreams that inspire us.

There are many models that reflect this tough reality. Let's present three of them:

- **Professional deadlock**

To illustrate a situation of professional deadlock, imagine you are starting a new job. After several years, you realize that there is no room for career development at a time when you don't know how to switch to a new career or job position. You realize that it is a dead-end and that you have to spend the rest of your life in the same role, with roughly the same salary and in the same company!

- **Limited demand**

This problem is also very widespread. You start a job in a company, let's say a distinguished position, and as the years go by, unlike professional deadlock, you climb the hierarchy of positions. After a few years you find yourself, for whatever reason, having problems with the company and seriously consider offering your resignation. You then realize, however, that there are few companies in need of your skills, and the positions that match your profile are filled. Here you find that the doors before you are closed and that you are stuck with same job in the same company, with all the compromises you may have to make.

- **End of the career life cycle**

Perhaps this example is less common than the previous two. You start off in a job that's in high demand and work your way up the hierarchal ladder. A few years later, however, due to economic, social, political, technological developments and changes, there is no more demand for your line of work. You find yourself without a job and don't know how to go about changing careers.

Barbara Grahn and Susan Maltz in their study "A Fork in the Road" estimate that, "70% of today's jobs [year 2003] will disappear by 2050"! This number seems very reasonable if we consider the rapid growth and breakthroughs we are witnessing in today's global economies, and if we realize that we are tighter in terms of change and transition from the industrial age to the age of knowledge and globalization.

1.3. But wait! It's Not Too Late

Even in the worst-case scenario there is still time. There's still hope, great hope indeed, as long as you have the willingness to change.

It is true that the road will not be easy if you want to make up for the past, but it is doable and can be very rewarding; all that is required of you is the desire to change and a clear path.

Let's refrain from focusing on specific mistakes from the past, as our tears won't bring it back... We mustn't look back and mourn the past; the road is still passable. We just have to identify it and walk the path.

Let's look ahead. There we will see what remains of our life, that which is worth our investing a bit of our effort, time and money, so we can orientate our lives towards happiness, especially as it usually takes no more than two years to reap and enjoy the fruits of our efforts.

Remember, it's not only your destiny you are deciding; rather it is that of all generations who will follow. Remember that the opportunities of your children, and their children after that, are clearly greater if you are successful, and the opposite is true if you are not!

Furthermore, remember that it is not only your destiny in this world alone, it is your destiny in the hereafter, too, and it is closely tied to the efforts that you exhibit in this world to rise and exalt yourself. This is what we are told in the Abrahamic religions, isn't it?

There are many models in which people with modest situations, whether mental, or material, at a later part of their lives, in a pivotal moment of determination, decide to change their destiny and course of their lives and succeed.

Miguel de Cervantes Saavedra, author of Don Quixote, which enchanted the world over 350 years ago, spent most of his life in a losing battle with debt and misfortune. He suffered a grave injury while at war, hampering his ability to use his left hand. Later in life, he occupied a number of governmental posts and was unsuccessful in all of them. He was imprisoned repeatedly, until something happened to him, which inspired him to write Don Quixote when he was 53 years old.

1.4. On the other hand

You may graduate from high school with modest grades that may not qualify for advancing into university, or it may force you to go into a degree that you are not interested in, one with no future. You may think your future is lost and that your life is doomed to failure, leaving you feeling frustrated.

But go easy on yourself! With a little effort, some focus, and sound planning, you can still change the course of your life in ways you never thought possible.

One day I met a young man who had recently earned certain high school qualifications, and he was feeling very down. He told me 'My life has slipped away before me". When I asked him why, I learned that he, because of family circumstances, had finished high school with grades too low to qualify him for a university placement. Furthermore, he didn't have sufficient financial resources to pay his own way.

I appeased him, for his life hadn't slipped away at all. All he needed to do was choose the right way to get out of his difficult situation, and this is what I helped him do in a long session planning his career path.

Don't be put off or give up; whatever your situation is, you can still change your life for the better. All you need to do is plan your career path and then pursue it!

2. Career Development Model

Before discussing how to plan your career, we need to understand the career development process and its components through the "Career Development Model".

This model demonstrates the ideal path for the career development process starting from the individual entering the business world and ending up with reaching the peak of the career pyramid.

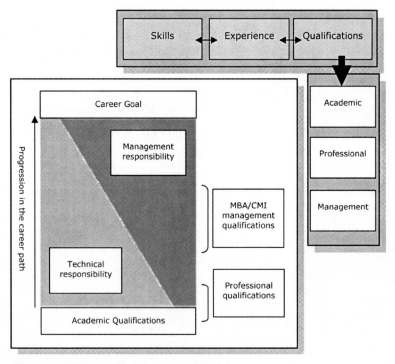

Figure 2/ Career Development Model

2.1. Academic qualifications:

An individual starts out on their career path, usually, based on the academic qualifications they hold.

Generally speaking, we can consider that a bachelor's degree is the minimum adequate level to begin the career path with. Although the career development path is not professionally associated with a bachelor's degree in numerous professions, the fact remains that many establishments still require a bachelor's degree as an essential condition for numerous professions particularly in the managerial sense. This may be due to what this qualification represents regarding cultural status on one side and the enormous and positive effects it has in broadening the human mind and opening scientific horizons on the other side.

Normally Master's and PhD degrees do not add much value in most non-academic/ research careers and professions. However, these qualifications can be seen in a lesser way if not supported by solid, firm and practical experience, by evaluating your capabilities in terms of the fear that these high academic qualifications may affect the practical side of your personality and render you purely theoretical and academic in tackling different issues you are expected to confront!

> In principle, we can consider that a bachelor's degree is the minimum adequate level to begin the career path

2.2. Career goal

We mean the career goal to be one of the highest positions at the peak of the job hierarchy that an individual might seek in their life, which can be achieved by advancing in that career from one position to a higher one.

Practically speaking, many may not reach these high positions; for some people the career goal may be represented in attaining and operating within modest administrative and professional jobs.

2.3. Progression in the career path:

In order to reach the peak of the job hierarchy (or the career goal you are seeking), you have to progress in the career from one job to another and from one position to another as this progression may provide you with knowledge, expertise and necessary skills to enable you perform well in your career goal.

In practice, there is no defined time span for the career path necessary to achieve your career goal, as this is restricted by many external and internal factors, one of which is the nature and particularity of the achievement you are seeking, another being your own capabilities and skills. Further factors include the effort you put into improving yourself to reach your goals, your relationships, the business environment around you and sometimes, your luck.

But what I can assure you is that your ability to achieve and perform is the major factor to reach your career goal and stay there.

> Make sure you change at least 3 jobs (establishments) through your progression towards your career goal to acquire "the adaptability" which can be counted as one of the talents necessary to possess in this age of knowledge/globalization

2.4. Technical responsibilities and managerial responsibilities:

Every job, at every level of the job hierarchy, usually entails technical and managerial responsibilities. Further to this, optimum performance in all types of jobs necessitate time management and management of available resources coupled with the required technical work.

The closer you progress towards executive positions, the more managerial responsibilities you have, in addition to more complicated, sensitive, and important technical responsibilities, however the time spent on technical responsibilities does becomes less. For example, an accountant's managerial responsibilities involve managing their own time, while their technical responsibilities include performing certain accountancy tasks. However, when promoted to the role of accounts supervisor, the managerial responsibilities are broadened to managing one's own time and the time of the accountants who report to the supervisor, whereas their technical responsibilities will still involve issuing financial and management reports.

This means that to get promoted to the position above your current role, you must be able to perform and deliver in the target position, which means you must be capable with both management and professional aspects. However, the most important element for climbing to the first line of a management position might be your ability to demonstrate your professional distinction, while you will also need to demonstrate your management competencies. This brings us to our next two points.

Strive to focus during the initial years in the job to gain profound, broad, professional experience. This is the cornerstone of your entire career path. It is costly and difficult to make repairs later on if you go through your first year/s on the job without gaining the appropriate professional experience and knowledge

2.5. Professional qualifications

By professional qualification, we refer to the international awards and qualifications in different specialization fields, which are recognition from internationally accredited professional boards/associations/institutes relating to an individual's ability to practice the profession. These qualifications are typically granted after one passes extremely difficult and complicated exams and attains the necessary experience and skills.

Not only does earning a professional qualification at the start of your career ensure that you have the required professional competence to practice your profession, it also proves you excel at it, giving you a competitive advantage over your colleagues and other applicants who do not possess professional qualification for management positions, particularly in the early stages.

These professional qualifications differ from academic qualifications in that they are developed by internationally known, chartered professional bodies, that are authorized to govern different professions, according to the competence of each body, develop and maintain their professional/ ethical standards and to develop the competency based practical skills, knowledge and understanding required in today's workplace, whereas academic qualifications are based on theoretical learning.

There are professional qualifications in most professions including medicine, engineering, training, marketing, accounting, insurance, human resources, many of which do not require the possession of a bachelor's degree to enter.

In most cases, demand for professional qualifications, along with the salaries paid for them, is much higher than purely academic qualifications in most professions. The demand for professional qualifications is constantly increasing in this age of knowledge/globalization.

> If possible, try to work towards passing professional qualification exams (that correspond to your career goal) starting in the second year of university, otherwise during the initial years in your job

2.6. MBA / CMI management qualifications

Being professionally accomplished is by no means sufficient to succeed in senior management positions; one must also possess the necessary management knowledge and skills. On this basis, obtaining an MBA or a CMI professional diploma in management is of the utmost importance should you aim to work in management positions, especially the most senior ones, not only because it affords you the necessary management competencies, but also because it proves, to a sizeable extent, that you possess these competencies.

The following is a brief overview of these qualifications:

- **MBA (Masters of Business Administration)**

The MBA is an academic degree in business administration that attracts a wide range of students from all academic

disciplines. The MBA originated in the United States, where its popularity spread in the late nineteenth century at a time when the country commenced with a curriculum specializing in business administration and promoted its use in factories and companies. Since then, the MBA has gained worldwide success and recognition.

- **CMI professional qualifications in management:**

This is an integrated set of management qualifications offered by the "Chartered Management Institute" (CMI) in the United Kingdom that enables you to achieve the title of "Chartered Manager". These professional qualifications stand out due to their focus on developing competency based practical skills, knowledge and understanding required in today's workplace, as opposed to academic qualifications based solely on theoretical knowledge.

- **The "Chartered Manager" status:**

The Chartered Manager Award is the ultimate accolade for practicing professional managers and is granted by the "Chartered Management Institute" (CMI) in the United Kingdom. It requires that you demonstrate how you have developed as a manager and how you have applied your leadership and change management skills to achieve significant business impact.

- **Chartered Management Institute (CMI), United Kingdom:**

CMI is the leading organisation for professional management in the UK. It was established over 50 years ago and consists of 89,000 individual members, 400 corporate members and 500 approved training centers.

CMI is responsible for promoting standards in management and acknowledges excellence through the awarding of recognised, professional qualifications, which lead towards "Chartered Manager" status.

After completing professional qualifications, and obtaining at least three years working experience, it is advisable to enroll in a MBA program at a distinguished university or to work on a CMI diploma in management to obtain the "Chartered Manager" status

2.7. The Ability of performance:

Based on the above, it becomes clear that the ability of achievement and performance is derived from having the right mix of three elements: qualifications (knowledge), experience and skills.

- **Qualifications:**

Qualifications represent the knowledge an individual requires to be able to achieve their career goal providing it is backed up by the necessary experience and skills.

Qualifications can be divided into three integrating types, each of which offers a different type of knowledge, way of thinking and approach to different situations:

- **Academic qualifications:** these include school education, bachelors, masters and doctorate education.

- **Professional qualifications:** as mentioned earlier

- **Management qualifications:** in reality, these are either academic qualifications, such as a MBA, or professional qualifications, such as CMI qualifications in management, as described earlier.

> Obtaining professional and academic qualifications is an important issue, but more important is acquiring the knowledge and skills these qualifications offer

- **Experience:**

This is the practical experience that one acquires during progression in their career path, which relates to their career goal. In reality, keeping a balance between the depth of experience and its comprehensiveness of the fields related to the career goal is a complicated process that requires profound professional knowledge of the career goal and its prerequisites. It is also linked to the circumstances of the job market (supply and demand), which might dictate that an individual embark upon a certain career path.

- **Skills and aptitudes:**

These are very crucial in regard to an individual's performance and achievement. There are two types: specialized skills, which are determined based on the career goal you aspire to, and general skills (aptitudes), which often are not directly related to the career goal. There are many types including entrepreneurship, leadership, independence, effective communication skills (written and oral), languages, innovation, creative thinking, analysis, teamwork, research and follow-up.

In fact, one of the main reasons why many of those who possess the required experience and qualifications fail is that they lack the appropriate skills.

Acquiring the relevant skills and aptitudes, generally, is much harder than acquiring the required experience and qualifications.

However, these skills and aptitudes can be acquired through personal effort, either within the job or outside the workplace. They can also be acquired in short professional and management training sessions and programs, for instance, offered by specialized institutes.

We have learned from our previous discussions regarding the "Career Development Model" that the two key fundamentals in the process of career planning are: firstly to identify a career goal and second, to determine a career path leading to this goal. In the following sections, we shall discuss this further, before considering some hypothetical cases.

> Using the "Career Development Model" correctly requires collecting the right and relevant information and taking the advice of specialists in the field

3. Outlining Your Career Goal

3.1. The importance of having a career goal

Setting yourself a career goal is very important as it is considered a fundamental factor in achieving success. The following is an illustration:

- Setting your career goal is pivotal in the process of planning your career path as it will direct and lead you to the job and position that really allows you to find yourself and to achieve your material and strategic ambitions, in addition to mapping out many of the other details and aspects of your life.

- Setting your career goal means adding a purpose to your life and giving measurable meaning to your movement and activity in life, making the process of developing yourself fun and clear whilst bringing you stability and happiness.

> Setting your career goal is pivotal to your success in life

3.2. When do we start outlining our career goal?

The process of identification of the career goal is essentially an ongoing process: it begins with early years of perception and realization (for example at age of 10) and lasts far into one's lifetime for as long as one has the will to think and change!

- **But why is it an ongoing process?**

Lifespan, especially in this age, is full of changes, whether the changes are at the level of the human being themselves, their perspectives, habits, desires and abilities, outer environment both local and global, socially, politically, economically, technically, culturally or other. These rapid changes inside the human existence or outside make it totally unrealistic for the individual to set a career goal and stick to it forever.

Therefore it is essential to review your career goal periodically to make sure it is what you are seeking to achieve, it is the goal that fulfils your desires, ambitions and perspectives towards life and focuses you to reach it. Should you discover otherwise, it is required that you amend or improve your career goal or even change it to become more appropriate to you and to the current and expected job market as will be discussed later.

However, try to stick to your career goal as long as you can. Try to avoid making changes to career goals that don't conform to your knowledge, expertise and skill capabilities. Frequent and unwarranted changes in the career goal may add unavoidable burdens to your life and drift you away from your real potential.

> Continuously review your career goal to ensure it is what you seek and that it is real and suitable. However, try to minimize your career goal changing processes as much as possible

- **Is it not too soon to begin determining your career goal during childhood?**

Humans move along their career paths through decisions they make and steps they take in their life, essentially starting at high school when they select some of the subjects they proceed to study. When selecting their university, their chosen major, then when selecting their first job after graduation, in time their options and opportunities begin to decrease as they walk the distance in their career paths.

However in reality, an individual can begin their walk towards their career goal at an early age of perception and realization in their childhood! To elaborate, let us recall the equation we discussed in the "Career Development Model": One's ability to reach to their career goal is determined by their ability to perform well in their job. However, an individual's ability to perform well is defined by their possession of the right combination of qualifications (knowledge), expertise and skills. We also mentioned that acquiring skills is generally harder than possessing expertise and qualifications.

The message here is that one can start acquiring the relevant skills required for their career goal during childhood! In fact, those skills that an individual acquires in their childhood can be more solid and effective than those they relatively acquire at an older age!

Consequently, starting to think about the career goal during childhood, with the help of the parents, inevitably would provide a person with a momentum to work on acquiring the suitable skills for their career goal through their younger years.

It is not only adults that have the need to live with objectivity in their lives, but also younger people: it gives a distinct meaning to their life, fills their free time with useful things as it is derived by their own motivations. It also restricts the feeling of the emptiness in their lives, which can have a devastating impact.

Here, we must emphasize that the role of parents (or counselor) is merely helping the child identify their career goal through initiating a conversation with them and displaying the choices before them according to related goal inputs and factors which will be discussed later in this book. It is not the place for the parents (or counselor) to determine the career goal on the child's behalf. It is not even their right to practice authoritative pressure towards the child to choose their career goal, even if they believe that it is right for them.

This does not mean that the parents should not practice parenthood towards their child to prevent them from taking a road that could ruin the child's life! What I am saying is that we have to help the child choose, if they choose any one of the generally accepted and reasonable goals such as teaching, medicine, engineering, computer science or others, we should not stand in their way or practice authoritative pressure to change their mind!

Let's not forget that a child is still a child; they do not face any decisive decisions at this stage of life, so there is no real damage around any acceptable goal that may be chosen at the time being! The importance of the child determining their goal lies in setting meaning, objectivity and motivation to their life, then sharpening their interests, improving themselves to acquire the skills they need for this goal, then protecting them from the free time and chaos which, unfortunately embraces a lot of our children, that in turn, leads them to delinquency in all its different shapes.

The first decisive decision the child will have to make is selecting their major which, won't be before they turn eighteen, which provides them with enough time to mature and make a decision of this kind, especially if the child is trained to think about their career goal, path and what surrounds them with regard to goal inputs from an early age with the help of their parents.

It occurred once that a member of the audience during one of my lectures I delivered in the field of planning the career path was a fifth-grade child (he was eleven). He came with his father and the child came to me a few days later after the lecture and said to me, 'you help many determine their career goals, and I also want you to help me determine my career goal'. I was really amazed at the time at the child's request. I thought it was just the flare up of enthusiasm but for an hour I tried to talk him out of it as he had many years to come before taking any steps that would enable him to take decisions relating to his career goal. However, I resigned to his persistence in the end. We had a lengthy discussion over a two-day span considering a selection of choices open to him. We discussed the different goal inputs that surrounded these choices until he ended up choosing computer networking as a profession, tentatively taking into consideration that this can be dramatically changeable in the future of his life due to the changes that could occur within him and also around him.

My time with him was up, but I knew later he convinced his parents to appoint a professional tutor in computer networking to teach him and I discovered he had bought a collection of used computers with his savings and with the help of his father for practice!

When I met his tutor around seven months after my meeting with the child, I discovered the child was doing well as he had finished the software programs A+ and N+. His next target was the international certificate CCNA "Cisco Certified Network Associate" in networks!

When I met the child once again I found him very enthusiastic: he decided to finish the CCNA during that school year and then practice higher professional qualifications one after another until he graduated from high school (grade 12), aiming at enrolling in a "commerce" major, whilst in conjunction with his university study, practice computer networking profession as a freelancer!

We cannot say this child is unique. However, he had a chance not too many children have as a whole! Let us try the same approach with our children, and I am sure we will have similar results.

> The process of determining a career goal at an early age provides the individual with the motivation and resourcefulness needed for acquiring relevant skills for their career goals. It also provides one with an insight and perspective in life

- **Is it a lifelong process?**

This process goes on far into one's lifespan for as long as they possess the will and the power to change and as long as they are able to think. There is no time limit for this process, even well into old age.

A distinguished writer in a local American newspaper, started to write at an age that exceeded ninety and continued her weekly columns until well after she reached one hundred years of age.

Another career success story focuses on an African American who grew up in a family of eight boys where he was the eldest. At the age of seventeen, he had to leave school and go to work to provide for his family.

He worked in construction, in a railway station, and then served in the army. For twenty years, he continued to work in truck manufacturing, in painting, welding and assembly lines in factories in Philadelphia, Pennsylvania.

In 1979, he was laid off from his work of welding aged forty-eight, at a time where he was a father of twelve children and a grandfather of seven grandsons! Despite the fact he was unable to tackle simple mathematical questions, he made up his mind to obtain a PhD degree in Information Technology!

He succeeded in tests that were the equivalent of high school exams and subsequently enrolled at Philadelphia College. There, he studied the entire educational curricula in Mathematics. In 1981, after he had obtained a degree from the College, he submitted an application to join Pennsylvania University.

At fifty-six, he was awarded a Bachelor's degree in Information Technology, after which he continued with his study to obtain a Master's degree and ended up with obtaining a PhD degree!

Unfortunately, it seems that in some cultures, people harbor a belief that one has to work hard in the early years of one's life to achieve their career goals before a certain age. Once that age is crossed, people with this attitude tend to relax and give in.

Even if you feel you have achieved your career goals you formed at the beginning of your working life and youth, you can and should determine more prestigious and ambitious goals, then seek to improve yourself and your capabilities towards reaching these goals. Should you achieve them, continue to make more and keep this an on-going process.

If you succeed to become a "financial controller" in a multinational company when you are sixty years old for instance, do not make this profession as an end to your motion and improvement in life! Think about the profession and positions higher than your current one, and then plan how to get that through improving yourself and your capabilities.

If you are a millionaire, and you own everything that makes you happy in this life: health, family, materialistic prosperity! Do not make these blessings the end of your life by quelling your motivation, motion and searching! Mankind resembles a horse in this situation: if its motion towards improvement and self-achievement ceases, its soul petrifies and dies!

It is not necessary for your goals to be personal, nor is your search purely for selfish gains; it would be wonderful to have goals that we can contribute, that make people around us happy.

> Career goal identification process is an ongoing process that never stops. It begins at the early years of perception and distinction but lasts until the final stage of life as long as one possesses the ability of thought and change!

3.3. How do we outline our career goal:

Identifying the career goal is the cornerstone of the process of planning your career path and formulating the details, and course of your life. You must therefore be cautious in determining your career goal and be reasonably certain that it concurs with your ambition and is within your reach.

Accordingly, once you determine your career goal, the following elements should be considered:

- Your internal constraints.

- The characteristics of the current and future job market.

- The observation of changes and ongoing review of the goal and path.

- The flexibility of the career goal, particularly in the early years.

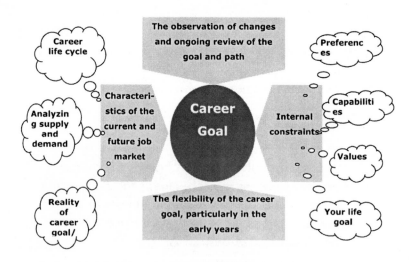

Figure 3 / Outlining your Career Goal

Next we shall shed light on these four elements:

- **Your internal constraints.**

These represent all of the constraints intrinsic to humans. It depends on your outlook on life, your character, moods, wants and abilities. These constraints directly affect, and are affected by, human behavior, movement in life coupled with feelings and sensitivities.

More specifically, we can break them down into four determinants:

- **your value:**

This is what stems mainly from your convictions and religious, social and political affiliations and which reflect your outlook on life in all its array of people, society, animals, and factors of life. For example, someone who is a member of the Humane Society for Animal Protection would find it difficult working in a meat factory, on a fish farm. Similarly, a person who is concerned and interested in preserving the environment would have a hard time working in factories and companies that emit high levels of pollution.

On the other hand, a person who believes they have certain messages for mankind or future generations may be eager to turn to teaching or to the media.

There are many determinants that can fall into the values category, such as risk/safety levels, flexibility, social services, independence, which influence that individual's beliefs into shaping their career goal, or even the job roles they may fill in their progression on the career path.

Outlining Your Career Goal

- **Your preferences and desires:**

These are not only related to the nature of the job roles in your proposed career path, such as capital or human, social or individual, office or field, etc, but also to the other effects you pay attention to. For example, you may consider medicine an enjoyable profession, but you dislike the system of working shifts or you may hate working in offices and enclosed spaces.

Therefore, it is very important that your career goal in all its merits (and the jobs you may encounter along your career path), affords you the utmost enjoyment and comfort and, at a minimum, does not irritate you or make you feel uncomfortable.

Don't forget that you spend over half of your daytime hours at work, so choosing a career that corresponds with your preferences will increase your productivity and happiness in your whole life.

- **Your capabilities (communication, leadership, speaking, analysis, etc.):**

The capabilities and skills you possess are one of the most important factors you should take into consideration when choosing your career goal.

As we mentioned earlier, the ability to perform well is determined by possessing the right combination of qualifications (knowledge), experience and skills, whereby the skills are the hardest to acquire. Therefore, we must be mindful that when choosing a career goal to select, the one that we possess already, to reasonable extent, is matching skills.

We may wish to teach, for example, and this fits our values. However, if we do not possess teaching skills and capabilities, perhaps we should choose a different profession and job role.

However, what happens if teaching is truly what you want to do in the end? Maybe it would fulfill your ambitions and coincide perfectly with your outlook on life. In this case you should choose teaching, even if this presents a serious challenge to acquire the skills required for teaching.

- **Your life goal:**

By life goal, we do not mean your desire to achieve material wealth, social standing and high-ranking positions, etc., as these are the general hopes and goals everyone strives for, in most cases.

What we mean specifically, are those special goals that some people set for themselves, and want to achieve them badly, perhaps at the expense of those general goals of comfort, status, wealth, etc. They may even make sacrifices to achieve these goals.

These goals may stem from a person's outlook on life and their beliefs, convictions and views. Maybe some bitter experiences a person lives through etch these goals in their mind. Maybe they are a result of other factors. A child whose father passes away before his eyes due to cancer, for example, may never be appeased until they find a cure for cancer and, as such, choose to make this a central part of their life goal.

In fact, the vast majority of people don't have particular goals for their life. However, if you happen to be one of those who do, you should be realistic and honest with yourself when setting them. You should also make sure your career goal is compatible with these special goals in a manner, and on a level, that is satisfying to you.

> You spend over half of your waken day at work, so your career goal and its path must match your values, desires, abilities and particular goals in life, to ensure optimum satisfaction and happiness

- **The characteristics of the current and future job market:**

The characteristics of the current job market, and those expected in the future, do not diminish the importance of our internal determinants in setting our career goals. These characters are external factors and influences that interact with peoples' internal determinants (internal factors) as they choose their career path and career goals.

We must therefore take these external factors and influences into consideration when we set our career goals and career paths. These characteristics are:

- **Career life cycle:**

A career is but a mere service product: it has a limited life cycle. The life cycle curve differs from one job/ career to another, depending on the social, cultural, economic, technological, financial, etc. circumstances and characteristics in local and international society. However, we can say that any job normally goes through the following four stages, from the time it appears in the job market to the time it no longer exists:

1. **Introduction Period:** This is the period in which the need for the job becomes apparent due to changes in the surrounding environment, be it social, cultural, economic, technological or other (we shall call them later "Environmental changes").

   Demand for the job/ career is usually low at this period. It is also risky because the position is likely to disappear from the job market and die in its infancy.

2. **Growth Period:** The job enters this period once it passes the introduction period. Demand begins to rise over time in this period. Currently, many professions can be placed in this category such as management consulting, audit management, business analysis, information systems management, etc.

3. **Maturity Period:** This is the period in which the rise in demand for the job begins to level off.

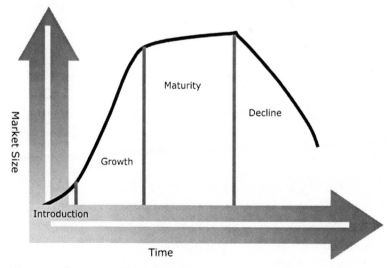

Figure 4 / Career Life cycle

4. **Decline Period:** This phase begins when demand for the job begins to subside. This is a common fate for many jobs due to an ever-changing environment. However, when the job reaches this phase, it can be catastrophic for the workers and employees in that job. Therefore, when any cultural, economic, or other signs/indicators emerge and point to the approach of this phase, we must begin to change our profession, perhaps to a similar one, but certainly more stable.

The characteristics of the life cycle curve of each job is different in terms of the expected duration at each of the four periods, the size of the anticipated job market at each period, and the slope degree of the curve at each period.

Financial Accounting and External Auditing has been in the maturity period for several decades, with a great level of demand, and this may last an additional number of years. On the other hand, industrial engineering, especially with regard to specific technological products, may pass through all four periods in only a few years, with very limited demand.

Furthermore, changes in the surrounding environment (social, cultural, economic, technological, etc.) may fundamentally change the characteristics of a job's life cycle curve and may shift it from one period to another in reverse order (from the maturity to growth stage, for example).

A good example of this is represented by high demand for HR professionals that was at maturity stage several years ago in the pre-technological age. However, due to advancement towards the knowledge and globalization age, with all the variables and challenges it generated and continues to generate, the importance of human capital and its sensitivity has increased tremendously. Accordingly, it can be said that the HR profession shifted back from the maturity period to the growth period, and demand for it will continue to increase for years to come before reaching the maturity period again.

It is therefore very important, both for identification of the career goal and mapping out the career path, that we keep an eye on the current characteristics of the life cycle curve relating to the goals that we are aiming for.

To identify these characteristics, I recommend that you speak with specialists in the field and seek their advice. You can also consult with accredited professional associations (such as those mentioned earlier) and read reports published on this topic.

> It is very important that we keep an eye on the current characteristics of the life cycle curve relative to the goals that we are aiming for

- Analyzing supply and demand

A job is like any other product; its price is determined at the point where supply and demand are equal. Based on this premise, it is not enough to assume that there is an increasing demand for a certain profession/job for us to believe that it has a promising future! We must also understand the current and the expected supply size of the job market.

Accordingly, if we find that the supply is greater than demand, then there are more candidates than positions, and your chances of succeeding will be reduced, slowing your procession towards your career goal.

Once again, it can become very complicated for people to find different statistical reports to determine the scope of their desired job's supply and demand. I therefore recommend that you speak with specialists in the field and seek advice from them. You can also consult with accredited professional associations (such as those mentioned earlier) and read reports published on this topic.

It is not enough to assume that there is an increasing demand for a certain profession/ job for us to believe it has a promising future! We must also understand the current and the expected supply size of the job market

-   **The path toward career goal and how realistic it is:**

This is the third external factor influencing how feasible it is to achieve our career goals.

To reach your goals, you will likely have to go through a series of other positions and gain certain knowledge, experience and skills related to your goal. We refer to this as "Progression in the career path".

However, what if your goal or path is not realistically within reach, either because of your personal circumstances and problems or those of the environment around you? For example, you would like to become a pilot, but you have vision problems, or a practicing surgeon, but there are no surgical hospitals in the region/town/country where you live.

- **The observation of changes and ongoing review of the goal and its path.**

As we mentioned earlier, life is full of changes, both within individuals and in their surroundings. These rapidly evolving changes have a powerful, direct effect on our career goals and their paths. Therefore, your goals and dreams today may not be the same as tomorrow, at which point there is no use in chasing them.

Furthermore, things don't always go as we would like, both in terms of our personal circumstances and the mechanisms and elements comprising our career path.

That is why; we need to review our goals to be sure that they are still subject to the factors we discussed earlier: the internal determinants and characteristics of the job market.

For example, you may have always wanted to be a teacher, but after a few years in the teaching field you realize you have changed and no longer feel like working with students. Or perhaps you feel a strong desire to start your own business, or you find the supply of teachers in the job market exceeds demand, exposing you to the risk of losing your job or not being able to meet your financial goals. In all such cases, it may be the perfect time for a career change, even if only to make you happier.

- **The flexibility of the career goal, particularly in the early years.**

This is the final element and it stems from the previous factor "The observation of changes and ongoing review of the goal and path". To be able to change your current career goal and path to another one depends greatly on your possession of the relevant competencies, skills, and knowledge that enable you to make the transition in a viable and realistic manner.

If you have been a surgeon, for example, and find yourself obligated to change your job, you may only have the option of staying in the medicine field, meaning the opportunities before you are few and limited. In comparison, if you have worked in the auditing domain, your transition possibilities would be relatively easier as you would have more alternatives to choose from.

What we do mean here by career goal flexibility is the level that it shares and corresponds with other career goals in its path's components and details. i.e the level of the similarities between their paths. The more flexible our career goal is, the more easily we will be able to switch from our current career to another.

Based on this premise, it is prudent that when choosing our career goal to make sure it is as flexible as possible, particularly in the early years of our career, when there is a relatively high possibility that our career goals will change, unless we are quite certain about our choice.

4. Career Planning Methodology

"Career Planning Methodology" is essentially based on the "career development model" and other theoretical concepts that we have discussed earlier. To begin with, we will explain this methodology, further to which we will move on to 2nd part of this book, where we will discuss the application of the methodology in various examples.

In accordance with this methodology, the career path is determined using the following six steps:

Figure 5 / Career Planning Methodology

45

4.1. Determine your career goal

As we have discussed in the previous section.

4.2. Determine required competencies -for achieving your career goal.

To facilitate this step you need to determine a competency's three elements. i.e. qualifications/ knowledge, experience and skills required for outstanding achievement and superior performance in your career goal.

In this step you will be required to determine professional and academic qualifications that you need obtain to perform well in your career. You also need to understand how important it is to obtain an MBA and/or to become a Chartered Manager. In terms of experience, you must determine what experience you need, in what fields, and how much in-depth experience you need. You must also be aware and understand the skills and aptitudes that you require to achieve and perform well your career goal.

We determine these three elements (qualifications/knowledge, experience and skills) on a theoretical basis. In practice, things are more flexible, simpler, and require fewer competencies for achieving your career goal, especially if we take in consideration the scarcity of well qualified resources.

If you possess a competency's three elements as described above, this will make you an attractive target for headhunters, and your competitive advantages are increased, making your career goal easier to attain. This also affords you added negotiating criteria for obtaining better salary packages.

For further details about a competency's three elements, qualifications/knowledge, experience and skills, refer to the previous discussion "career development model".

> Determine a competency's three elements. i.e. qualifications/ knowledge, experience and skills required for outstanding achievement and superior performance in your career goal

4.3. Analyze your existing competencies: Define what you already possess with regard to a competency's three elements, which, conform, to your career goals.

Acquiring a competency's three elements of achievement does not happen overnight, and is not something you can come by through a training program or several programs, which you may attend! What we hear sometimes in the training market about the existence of quick and effective solutions is incorrect, or else there would not be scarcity in the qualified and outstanding human resources staff!

At the same time, you do not have to be a superhero or born gifted to acquire these competencies!

All that you require is to be an average person in terms of your capabilities, yet be committed to improving yourself and seeking to acquire these three elements of achievement through your years of progression in a specific career path. This essentially sets a target for yourself that will lead you to acquiring the necessary capabilities and competencies that form and structure your path towards reaching your career goal.

How can I plot this path? This is what we are going to discuss. After we have defined the targeted prerequisites in this path which are the three elements of achievement you need to possess to reach your career goal, the next step is to determine the first section of the path, namely your position on that path, in other words determining what we actually possess in regard to qualifications, expertise and skills which conform with our career goal.

4.4. Determine requirements to fill gaps - between what you actually possess in terms of competencies and what is required to be developed to achieve your career goal.

Realizing what you actually possess in regard to suitable skills and competencies on one hand, and what it takes from you to achieve your career goal on the other hand enables you to specify the gaps, whether it be related to the level of qualifications, experience or the level of skills and talents.

Identification of these gaps, which require to be filled through your career path, enables you in turn to specify the requirements to fill these gaps aimed at acquiring the targeted competencies.

For example, it is not enough to say I need a professional qualification in accounting! You need to decide which one specifically? From which country and what are its requirements? Do you meet these requirements to enroll in the course? Do you have the resources to do this qualification? Are there other alternatives to this qualification? What is the extent of preference of these alternatives?

4.5. Determine your career path - that allows you to fill the gaps and arrive at your career goal.

Filling the gaps and meeting the requirements you identified in step four often takes several years. Fulfilling them successfully depends on your competencies and skills, your career goal, the amount of effort, time and focus you invest and a number of other factors.

However, it is equally true that you will not be able to meet all these requirements at once. You must achieve them at various stages along your career path in an effective, realistic and practical manner in accordance with your financial, social and other circumstances, provided it ensures you reap greater returns and satisfaction in the short and long term.

To illustrate my point, let us suppose a high school student in a relatively difficult financial situation is aiming to run his own financial investment business on an international level as this would bring him a sense of enjoyment, an elevated financial position, and independence.

To plan his career path, he takes all of the aforementioned steps. Now, at the fifth step, in which he identifies his career development path and seeks to achieve necessary requirements during the years of his planed career path, he proceeds as follows:

Year	Age	Planned action
2009–2013	18-22 years	• Bachelor's degree in accounting from a local, recognized, university in evening classes. • Works in accountancy field in the mornings to finance university tuition fees and CPA exam after graduation.
2013–2014	22-23 years	• Time set aside for preparing for CPA exam.

Career Planning Methodology

Year	Age	Planned action
2014–2017	23-26 years	• With CPA certificate, works in new well-paid position in financial investment for a distinguished international investment firm with a view of gaining profound, pertinent experience in the field. • Studies for American Certified Financial Analyst (CFA) qualification. • Saves enough money to set aside time for an MBA program.
2017–2018	26-27 years	• Time set aside for studying for the MBA in the field of investment at one of the world's most recognized universities for that field.
2018–2021	27-30 years	• Works in a key position (assistant manager, for example) in financial investment for an international investment firm in a developed foreign country to gain international experience in investment. • Works his way up until reaching the position of investment manager in the same firm or similar organization.
2021–2023	30 - 32 years	• Works as head of investment or general manager of investment in a prominent local firm to update local investment experience and to get familiar with customer network and local investment laws, for the purpose of research and groundwork with regard to starting his own business.
2023- ?	32-?? years	• Starts own business at an international level in the financial investment field.

4.6. Monitoring the variables, periodical reassessment and re-planning

"Easier said than done" "Unrealistic..." "Life doesn't always go as we plan..." Comments like these are what I expect to hear from those who have read what I've said about the five steps – and they are quite true!

Every day, life proves that it isn't stable at all! You make your plans judiciously and get yourself organized in a highly realistic and practical manner, only to find that something unexpected comes along and throws all your plans to the wind! This can happen over and over again. Maybe it's your mistake because your planning is unrealistic, or because you neglected a few important factors. Or maybe it's because of other factors which have nothing to do with you and which are beyond your will or control.

Such is life. This is part of life's reality, and we must take this into account when planning. We must be ready for these surprises both on a mental and practical level.

Add to this the aforementioned continuous, tremendous and rapid changes that affect our surroundings, whether they are economic, political, social, technological, and so forth, it highlights that there are certainly numerous factors which can have a direct impact on our plans and goals.

Therefore, in order to achieve your career goals, you must constantly review and observe the variables and changes, which affect your surroundings, or you personally. This requires periodical re-assessment of your career path, how well you are able to follow it, and how realistic it is in order to adjust and develop your goals and career path to make them more realistic and congruent with your life's circumstances and your particularities, and to make them more effective and efficient.

Let us suppose, for example, that the student we mentioned earlier had planned to get married at the age of 26, just before traveling with his wife to start his MBA abroad.

In reality, though, he gets married right after his graduation and moves into his own home. Perhaps he does so in response to pressures from his family, or as a response to his own urgent needs, or for other reasons originally unintended.

Now, this marriage changes matters significantly for his career, and he must readjust to be able to reach his career goal in a practical, effective way. Let's say he fully understands that he cannot study for the CPA for an entire year as planned as he cannot set aside the necessary time, attention, and devotion in light of his new family responsibilities, combined with the responsibilities of his current job.

This directly and adversely affects his ability to get the job in financial investment he had originally targeted because he won't possess the competitive advantage he had planned for (CPA).

In this situation, he could decide not to study for the CPA and, instead, begin studying for the CFA in conjunction with his current job, thus freeing up time. Passing modules in the CFA program can still afford him a competitive advantage that could help him considerably in achieving his ideal job in a prominent international investment firm thus still being able to continue pursuing his initial plan.

4.7. Highlights on applying the methodology

- **Plan your career yourself**

There is no single, correct path to your career goal, and alternative paths are not necessarily wrong. There are relative matters which vary from one person to another based on their competencies, interests, dedication, relationships, networks, luck, goals, opinions, circumstances, actual and expected characteristics of the job market and the laws and situation of the country they live in, in addition to many other factors. That is why the views of specialists may differ significantly, in terms of the details of career path particularities, when it comes to applying the methodology in practice.

You must therefore make your decision and map out your plan according to your own convictions, but only after consulting with specialists.

Let us presume that the student in step 6 from the previous example was lucky and found a job he strived for in the field of financial investment with a prominent international investment company, despite the fact he had no clear competitive advantage, other than his characteristics and opportune circumstances. At this point, he might see that it is more viable for him not to do the CFA and instead immediately start studying his MBA in investment from a distinguished international business school through E-learning rather than traveling abroad! He could be right and this may lead him to attain his career goal in a shorter, much simpler and easier approach.

You are in the best position to understand yourself and identify your competencies and needs, as well as your surroundings and tendencies. You are the one who will reap the consequences of your actions and you are the only one accountable for them and responsible for them. So make your own decisions and don't let anyone, even your own parents, decide for you or put pressure on you to proceed in a direction you don't believe in or want.

- **Be realistic**

You are not the only who promotes and imposes your own will in this life! The whole world, with all of its components and fundamentals moves, prescribes and shapes life as we see it. With regard to your actions and movements in this life, others can influence this, as can what life components surround you, as their movements and actions affect you and what you do in both positive and negative ways. We must have a firm grasp of this notion when we map out our career path and trajectory in life in general.

There are many social, economic, political, technological and even natural factors that influence our actual journey through life, what we do and what we strive to do. These factors are constantly changing very rapidly, particularly in this age of knowledge and globalization in which we live. This means that there are no definitive results for what we do when we move toward our goals and through our life in general. There are only possibilities and trade-offs!

For example, there is nothing to guarantee that the student, in our pervious example, will attain the job he is looking for in the field of financial investment, even after obtaining the CFA qualification and gaining other required experience. Even if we assume there are vacant positions, and that he is the most highly qualified individual for the job, he might not be selected because the director is unconvinced as to his ability, or perhaps the executive director wishes to appoint one of his relatives, or indeed for a multitude of reasons!

On the other hand, he might be selected the job, even without possession of relevant qualification or experience even though there are other more qualified applicants! This could happen for one reason or another and they might even not be apparent, perhaps because the executive director saw potential in him that he didn't see in himself.

As we said earlier, this is very realistic, and we must always keep our eyes open and be mentally ready to deal with these situations and frustrations in a positive way.

The following are a few words of advice to help you confront situations like these in a more positive manner:

- **Strive and plan for the best, but be ready for the worst:**

Though it may be true that the chances of things going wrong may be slim if you have planned well, things can still go wrong and the worst-case scenario might happen, so you must be ready.

Evaluate the worst-case scenario fully, either before or after it happens, and you will find most of the time that it's not so bad in itself. It might even be a good thing, as negatives can invariably be turned into positives, only not if compared to what you expected, planned for and deserved!

- **Exhibit perseverance and b˜e ready for challenge**

You may fail once, or many times, but you must exhibit perseverance and be ready for a challenge. The difficulty of achieving success is what sets apart successful persons and makes the success pleasurable.

If distinction and success were easy, there would be many successful people, and competitive advantage over others would cease to exist.

In fact, you don't need to be superhuman to be successful and to stand out from everyone else. All you need is a clear path and a fighting and persevering spirit.

It is true that failure, especially early in your life, can mean losing some essential needs in life, such as security and it could make your life more difficult until you get yourself out of the situation. However, the only way to eradicate those problems is to succeed. So hang in there and give it your all until you rescue yourself and your dependents. Then, don't stay idle, keep striving to succeed until you achieve more than what you were aiming for.

- **Be flexible enough to change your path or goal in line with changes in the associated factors.**

Practicing in life, cogitation, and consulting educated people around you, is what you need to learn how to adapt your movement in this world to the life around you, and to your circumstances. You have to know when you have to hold fast and when you have to change, when you have to persevere, when to be silent and observe, and when to attack hard with everything you have! Call it war and struggle with life, or call it a dance with life, it's all the same. However, do it with enjoyment.

Observe the plant growing in the river: if it weren't flexible it would crash into the water bombarding it!

The unforeseen happens and your plans fail... Do not stop at this point and lament it - think beyond... Get your papers back in order, re-examine your talent, get advice from those you trust around you, and then modify your path or your goal in accordance with your convictions.

Suppose in our previous example you are in the position of the student. You have been awarded the CPA qualification and then found an excellent job in the field of financial investment with a prestigious investment firm. After months of hard work and successful performance, and the satisfaction of your direct manager, a personal problem arises between you and the Executive Director of the firm. Accordingly, the firm puts great pressure on you, making your life in the organization miserable, ultimately forcing you to resign! You tried to solve the problem with the firm and the Executive Director but you were not successful.

This situation is of course bad, but it is reality and you have to deal with it! Think of the options available to you: staying with the firm means suffering psychological pressure, in addition to the possibility of not passing the CFA exam. The initial choices available to you are:

- Stay with the firm, gaining as much professional experience as possible, speeding up your plans to travel to study for the MBA, and leaving the CFA for another time.

- Search for another job in the same area, but with another firm, perhaps even outside the country, and then proceed with the path you had mapped out earlier.

Whilst looking for another job, you are offered an excellent job in the field of financial and management consulting with a distinguished international firm, permitting you in the long run to start your own management and financial consulting business.

You have to stop here and re-assess the situation. Is your goal in the long-term to run your own business in financial investment, or run your own business regardless of whether it is in financial investment, management consulting or any other professional field?

You need the flexibility to be able to deal with your new situation and make the right decision appropriate for you.

By showing flexibility in re-shuffling your cards, plans and priorities, according to changes in the associated elements and factors, you gain the ability to deal positively with reality and all its variables!

Part Two

Models
and Applications

Introduction

For further clarification on how to apply the methodology of career planning, we shall present a series of different examples and attempt to apply the method in each case. The following represents the different models:

- **The standard model,** in which we shall take the example of an average individual who graduates with a university degree in the specialization he intends to work in.

- **Deviation from the university specialization** represents an example of a person who has a certain specialization but who chooses to aim for a job in another specialization.

- **Inability to complete university study.** This example involves an individual who was unable to gain admission into university because he graduated from high school with a low average that does not qualify him for research or a grant and who cannot finance his university studies.

- **Career planning at a later age.** In this case, the example involves a person who decided at a relatively late stage in life to plan his career path.

However, before beginning discussions and planning the hypothetical career path in these situations, I will repeat what I have said earlier: There is no one correct path. These matters are highly relative, just as each individual differs from others and their circumstances.

1. Standard Model:

Let us assume that you wish to specialize your job role in the same field as your university degree and that you are now planning your career path. Now we will discuss the methodology and its application in this particular scenario:

1.1. Step one: Determine your career goal

Further to identifying and becoming familiar with your internal constraints and studying the job market, let's assume you decide that your career goal is to become "Head of Internal Audit" for a major multinational organization.

1.2. Step two: Determine required competencies for achieving your career goal

To be able to achieve your career goal, you must possess a set of professional and management skills that we can summarize as follows:

- **Educational and professional qualifications:**

- From an academic perspective:

You need to possess a bachelor's degree, preferably in accounting.

- From a professional perspective:

Although the American Certified Internal Auditor (CIA) qualification could be the most relevant specialized certificate, the job market also accepts the American Certified Public

Accountant (CPA) and British Chartered Accountant (CA or ACCA) certificates.

Moreover, as the internal auditor's work is closely linked to internal consultancy tasks, it is preferable that they possess the British Diploma in Management Consultancy (DMC) or even the international "Certified Management Consultant" (CMC) certificate.

- **From a management perspective:**

To be qualified to lead internal auditing, you must possess the necessary management abilities and skills, owing to the fact that you are expected to lead teams of auditors.

To acquire these management skills, or to prove to the employer you have them, you must either earn the academic MBA or a CMI qualification in management.

However, it should be noted that, nowadays, perhaps due to a shortage of professionally qualified executives, and perhaps because of limited public awareness of the job market, these management qualifications are not considered essential, even if you take into account the added advantage for attaining the position of Head of Internal Audit.

▪ **The necessary professional and management experience:**

It is difficult to give specific, quantified figures regarding the number of years experience required, as this is a relative matter. It depends greatly on a person's abilities and their degree of focus, concern and motivation.

Nevertheless, generally speaking, we can say that the experience required to achieve this career goal is around ten years of in-depth, varied experience, of which roughly seven years are spent in the field of internal and external auditing, and no less than two years as internal audit manager. It is also preferable that at least three of these years be spent working in one of the reputable auditing firms.

- **Skills and aptitudes:**

There are many skills and aptitudes required for any career goal to be successful, which is why it is desirable to focus on the most important ones, particularly those needing the most improvement. Let's suppose in our case that the most important skills required are: written and oral skills, problem solving, numeric skills, listening skills, analytical skills and social skills.

We need to be able to work with this data more effectively, so I suggest that we start by listing them in a table as follows:

Step two: Determine required competencies	
Qualifications	**Academic:** Bachelor's, preferably in accounting. **Professional:** CIA, CPA, or CA, preferably coupled with "Diploma in Management Consultancy" (DMC). **Management:** MBA or CMI Executive Diploma in Strategic Management and Leadership (EDSML), but not essential.
Experience	Around 10 years, roughly 7 of which are in internal and external auditing, 2 as internal audit manager, and preferably at least 3 of which are spent in a reputable international auditing firm.
Skills	Written and oral skills, problem solving, numerical skills, listening skills, analytical skills and social skills.

1.3. Step three: Analyze your existing competencies

Now, after determining the professional and management abilities required for your career goal, you must determine to what extent you possess these abilities, in terms of qualifications, experience and skills. Let's assume you are in your second year of your bachelor's degree in accounting. When trying to identify which of the necessary skills you possess, you find that you possess those listed below:

Step three: Analyze your existing competencies	
Qualifications	**Academic:** Second year of bachelor's accounting program **Professional:** none **Management:** none
Experience	None
Skills	**Strengths:** Communication and listening/math and numbers/analysis. **Weakness:** writing skills

1.4. Step four: Determine the requirements to fill gaps between what you actually possess in terms of competencies and what is required for your career goal.

When doing this, you must take your abilities and circumstances into account. For example, you can't decide to study for the CPA exam if you are from a country whose citizens are unable to obtain entry visas to the United States, as the centers that administer these exams are only located there.

- **Educational and professional qualifications:**

- **From an academic perspective:**

You need to complete your bachelor's degree in accounting.

- **From a professional perspective:**

Once you have compared the different professional qualifications required (as mentioned earlier, CPA, CIA, or ACCA), let's say you decide to prepare for the CPA certificate with a view to being able to work in a recognized international auditing firm.

Furthermore, you feel that you possess the required knowledge to pass the four CPA exams at the first attempt and then obtain the certificate within 6 months of starting the studies.

To gain a competitive advantage over others who have professional qualifications in internal auditing, you decide to try to obtain the British DMC diploma.

- **From a management perspective:**

As both qualifications: the MBA and CMI Executive Diploma in Strategic Management and Leadership (EDSLM) are both relatively easy to obtain, you decide to leave the matter of studying one of the two to a later date, at a point where you wish to pursue studying for a management qualification.

- **The necessary professional and management experience:**

In order to acquire in-depth, hands-on and varied experience in auditing, you also decide to start working with one of the prominent international auditing firms for a period of three years and then work your way up the hierarchy until you reach your desired position.

- **Skills and aptitudes:**

You need to hone your writing skills, among other skills (professional and general), which, you will identify later as you are working.

Let us place the results from step four in a table to clarify them completely:

Step four: Determine requirements to fill gaps	
Qualifications	**Academic:** Bachelor's in accounting. **Professional:** CPA and DMC **Management:** MBA or EDSML
Experience	As identified in step two, but start working with a prominent international auditing firm for about 3 years.
Skills	You mainly need to hone your writing skills, along with other skills (professional and general), which, you will identify later as you are working. You will develop these skills along your career path.

1.5. Step five: Determine your career path that allows you to fill the gaps and arrive at your career goal.

In this step, you will identify your career development path and strive to attain the requirements for filling the gaps, as identified in step four, as you progress along your career path as follows:

Step five: Determine your career path		
Year	**Age**	**Planned action**
2009-2011	20-22 years	• Finish bachelor's degree in accounting, • Study for the American CPA exam.
2011-2014	22-25 year	• Work in a prominent international audit firm (capitalizing on the competitive advantage you have: the CPA).
2014-2016	25-27 years	• Work as a senior internal auditor in any distinguished organization. • Study for DMC diploma
2016-2019	27-30 years	• Transfer to another company as internal audit manager • Study for MBA or CMI Executive Diploma in Strategic Management and Leadership (EDSMLM).
2019- ?	30-?? years	• You are now qualified to achieve your career goal to work as "Head of internal audit" for a major multinational organization"

Let us also present the results in chart form as follows:

1.6. Step six: Monitoring the variables, reassessment and re-planning periodically

Let us assume, for example, that during your work as a chief internal auditor (years 2014-2016), you decide for some reason to change your career goal to "Group Executive Vice-President of Financial Affairs" or "Partner in a management consulting firm". The questions raised here are, how to change this career path of yours and what must you do to transfer to the new one?

- **Changing the goal to "Group Executive Vice-President of Financial Affairs":**

As a general rule, to be able to switch careers, you must possess the capabilities (qualifications, experience and skills) to sell yourself in the job market in your new chosen field.

Applying this rule to our present case, we can say that, despite your excellent experience in accounting, auditing and related fields, your natural readiness to excel in financial matters, your prior experience and qualifications, your actual experience in high-level financial affairs is limited. This could hinder you in trying to land that position related to executive financial affairs.

To alleviate this predicament, you must try to proceed with this transition towards higher-level financial affairs, either in your current firm or another one. At the same time, you must begin studying for an MBA in financial affairs. This will position you better to make that transition and gain promotion to the level of Director of Financial Affairs in a relatively shorter timescale.

By making this transition and gaining the promotions, you are now on the right track, one that will lead you, if you plan well, to your goal of becoming "Group Executive Vice-President of Financial Affairs of the group".

- **Changing to the goal "Partner in a management consultancy firm":**

Although external auditing experience is far removed from the experience required for management consultancy, other tasks auditors typically perform, particularly in internal auditing, are closely related to management consultancy.

Therefore, remaining in your position, as "Senior Internal Auditor" does not distract your efforts to switch to a management consultancy role, given that the experience is by no means irrelevant.

However, owing to the limited number of positions in management consultancy, you must have a competitive advantage that enables you to enter this realm. The competitive advantage can be gained through achieving a DMC diploma (or CMC qualification).

By making this switch to internal or external management consultancy, obtaining the DMC qualification and obtaining the international CMC qualification, you are now on the right track towards attaining your goal, if your planning is done properly, of becoming a "Partner in a management consultancy firm".

2. Deviation from the University Specialization

In the previous example (the standard example), we assumed you want to specialize in the same university major, but what happens if you to specialize in another field other than your university major?

Let us discuss the same previous example. This time we will assume you are studying in the Engineering Faculty, but after you became a sophomore you decided to change your career goal to be, as we mentioned in the previous example "Head of internal audit" for a major company or group of companies, at a time where you could not change your university specialization.

2.1. The first three steps

We will not repeat the discussion with regard to the first three steps, as there is almost no change from the standard example. We will therefore move to the fourth step.

2.2. Step four: Determine requirements to fill gaps
between what you actually possess in terms of competencies and what is required for your career goal.

- **Educational and professional qualifications:**

- **From an academic perspective:**

You need to complete your bachelor's degree, even if it is not in accounting. However, you are required to study Accounting, either as a minor specialization or a professional training programme.

- **From a professional perspective:**

You cannot study the certified public accountant (CPA) qualification at present due to time constraints. Moreover, you might think that CA is not a practical choice, due to the long duration of the program.

Therefore, maybe the only option open to you is to study the certified internal auditor (CIA) qualification. In general, the CIA qualification could be relatively easier, faster and less expensive compared with CPA or CA qualifications.

To possess the competitive edge against other professional qualified people in internal auditing, you can also seek to obtain the British Diploma in Management Consultancy (DMC).

- **From a management perspective:**

As both qualifications: the MBA and CMI Executive Diploma in Strategic Management and Leadership (EDSML) are relatively easy to obtain, you decide to leave the matter of choosing one of the two to a later date, at a point where you decide to pursue a management qualification.

- **The necessary professional and management experience:**

To obtain the profound, professional and diverse expertise of auditing, as specified in the second step in the standard model, you decide to work for one of the international renowned auditing firms for three years, and then progress in various careers towards your career goal.

Although the CIA qualification has certain esteem in the labor market, it may not be considered to give the most competitive edge likened with CA or CPA in obtaining a job of an auditor in an internationally renowned auditing firm, so you may have to compromise on salary to obtain the job you want for at least one year to acquire the necessary experience.

Deviation from the University Specialization

After obtaining one years experience, in addition to what you possess in terms of knowledge and qualifications, you are in the perfect situation to obtain the best available job opportunities in such renowned international auditing firms along with the appropriate salary level.

- **Skills and talents:**

You have to improve your writing skills in addition to other skills (professional and general) defined later through the line of work.

We can now put the results we have gathered in the fourth step into a table as follows:

Step four: Determine requirements to fill gaps	
Qualifications	**Academic:** finishing the B.A in Engineering + Accounting (either as a minor or a professional training programme). **Professional:** CIA and the British Diploma in Management Consultancy (DMC). **Management:** MBA or the CMI Executive Diploma in the Strategic Management and Leadership (EDSML).
Expertise	As specified in the second step in the standard model, start to work for one of the internationally renowned auditing firm for a year at a reduced salary level, then two years for one of the internationally renowned auditing firms.
Skills	You have to improve your writing skills in addition to other skills (professional and general) defined later through the line of work. These skills will be improved throughout your career path.

2.3. Step five: Determine your career path that allows you to fill the gaps and arrive at your career goal.

In this step, we will determine your career path improvement and define the necessary requirements to fill the gaps, determined in the fourth step, over the span of your virtual career path as follows:

Step five: Determine your career path		
Year	**Age**	**The procedure to be taken**
2009 – 2011	20 – 22 years	▪ Finishing the B.A in Engineering. ▪ Study Accounting. ▪ Study CIA qualification
2011 – 2012	22 – 23 years	▪ Work for a renowned international auditing firm at entry level with reduced salary.
2012 – 2014	23 – 25 years	▪ Work for a renowned international auditing firm at enhanced level with higher salary.
2014 – 2016	25 – 27 years	▪ Work as a senior internal auditor at any renowned organization. ▪ Study the Diploma in Management Consultancy (DMC).
2016 – 2019	27 – 30 years	▪ Transfer to another company as internal audit manager. ▪ Study MBA or CMI Executive Diploma in Strategic Management and Leadership (EDSML).
2019 - ????	30 - ?? years	▪ You are now qualified to achieve your career goal as "chief internal auditor for a major company or a conglomerate", either in the firm you work for or in another one.

Deviation from the University Specialization

We put these results in a diagram as follows:

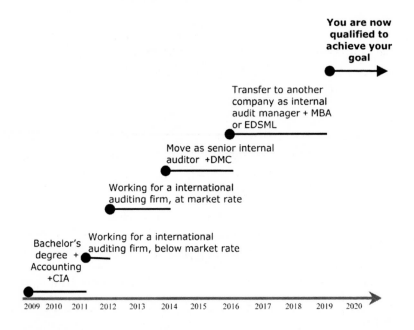

3. Inability to Complete University Study

Graduating from high school with low grades may not qualify you for obtaining a university grant, and you may not be able to finance your university studies due to financial hardship. Overcome with frustration, you may think that your future is lost and that your life is doomed to fail.

But go easy on yourself! With a little effort, some focus, and sound planning, you can still change the course of your life in ways you would never think possible.

Let us explore how the methodology can be applied to this example so that this change can be facilitated.

3.1. Step one: Determine your career goal

Suppose that, after identifying your internal constraints, becoming familiar with them and studying the job market, you decide that your career goal is to become an "IT manager in a large company"

3.2. Step two: Determine required competencies for achieving your career goal

To be able to achieve your career goal, you must possess a set of professional and management skills that we can summarize as follows:

- **Educational and professional qualifications:**

- From an academic perspective:

You need to have a bachelor's degree, preferably in computing/ information systems.

- From a professional perspective:

It is assumed that there is a strong demand in the job market for those who possess professional qualifications in project management (such as the American PMP degree) for IT manager positions.

- From a management perspective:

You may plan to study for MBA in IT or Management Information Systems.

- **The necessary professional and management experience:**

As mentioned earlier, it is difficult to specify the exact number of years of experience required, as this is a very relative matter. It depends greatly on a person's abilities and their degree of focus, concern and motivation.

Nevertheless, generally speaking, we can say that the experience required to achieve this career goal is around five to seven years of in-depth, varied experience, in the field of IT management and management information systems.

- **Skills and aptitudes:**

Let's suppose in our case that the most important skills required are: communication, problem solving and analytical skills.

We need to be able to work with this data more effectively, so I suggest that we start by listing them in a table as follows:

Step two: Determine required competencies for achieving your career goal	
Qualifications	**Academic:** Bachelor's degree, preferably in IT/information systems. **Professional:** Professional qualification in Project Management. **Management:** MBA in IT or Management Information Systems.
Experience	5-7 years of varied experience in the fields of information systems and IT.
Skills	Written and oral skills, problem solving, analytical skills.

3.3. Step three: Analyze your existing competencies

Let's suppose that, when trying to identify which of the competencies you possess, you find that you have those listed below:

Step three: Analyze your existing competencies	
Qualifications	**Academic:** high school **Professional:** none **Management:** none
Experience	None
Skills	**Good:** analysis.

3.4. Step four: Determine requirements to fill gaps
between what you actually possess of competencies
and what is required for your career goal.

- **Competitive advantage "your key to the solution":**

We determined in step two that you must obtain a bachelor's
degree in IT / management information systems, but the
problem is you can't afford university studies.

To solve this problem, you can enroll in evening courses while
working during the day to finance your studies. However, it
has become a fact of life in many countries that the salary of
an employee with only a high school degree is comparatively
low and not enough to pay university tuition.

Add to this, the fact is that you are aiming to work in the
field in which you wish to specialize and which has been the
focus of your academic career, which typically lasts four to
five years, in order to gain the work experience required to
achieve your career goal.

Perhaps in the past there was no solution to this predicament,
but today matters have changed. The solution may simply lie
in finding what "competitive advantage" you have that may
open the door to the desired job in your area of specialization
and with a salary that exceeds that of a high school graduate
several times over, or maybe even that of a university
graduate!

This advantage can be acquired by gaining the right
professional qualification in your specialization area and
thereby unlocking the door to the job market. What we mean
by the right professional qualification is the qualification
where you fulfill its pre-requirements. i.e. one that does not
require, for example, that you firstly obtain a bachelor's

degree. Moreover, you can acquire it in approximately a year's time for relatively little money, with the resulting qualification being well accepted in the job market and in demand.

> The key lies in acquiring the right professional qualification in your specialization area and thereby unlocking the door to the job market - and at the right salary!

However, do such qualifications exist? The answer is yes, but you just have to be sure they exist in your desired specialization. Otherwise you should change this specialization to the closest possible field to ensure being able to complete your university studies. After that, you can review your career path towards reaching your career goal.

If an individual in this predicament wants to become a "Group Executive Vice-President of Financial Affairs". In this case one would need to study and obtain the American "Certified Management Accountant" certificate (CMA) since this does not require a bachelor's degree and is highly accepted in the job market. At the same time, it can be obtained in less than a year time and at a reasonable cost.

Referring to our current example, I would recommend the CCNA (Cisco Certified Network Associate) certification. This certification is widely accepted in the job market, and again you can complete it in less than a year, at a reasonable cost. Holding the CCNA certification will permit you to find a reasonable IT job with a good salary, enough to cover your university studies.

Accordingly, we can identify the requirements for filling the gaps between the skills and abilities you have and those needed for your career goal in following ways:

- **Educational and professional qualifications:**

  - From an academic perspective:

Bachelor's degree in IT/information systems.

  - From a professional perspective:

Professional qualification in Project Management (such as the American PMP) and the CCNA.

  - From a management perspective:

MBA in IT or information systems.

- **The necessary professional and management experience:**

5-7 years of varied experience in the fields of information systems and IT.

- **Skills and aptitudes:**

Written and oral skills, problem solving, numerical skills, listening skills, analytical skills and other professional and general skills to be determined later while you are working.

Let us place the results from step four in a table to clarify them completely:

Step four: Determine requirements to fill gaps	
Qualifications	**Academic:** Bachelor's degree in IT. **Professional:** PMP + CCNA **Management:** MBA in IT or information systems.
Experience	5-7 years of varied experience in the fields of information systems and IT.
Skills	Communication skills, problem solving, numerical skills, listening skills, analytical skills and other professional and general skills to be determined later while you are working.

3.5. Step five: Determine your career path that allows you to fill the gaps and arrive at your career goal.

In this step, we will determine your career path improvement and define the necessary requirements to fill the gaps, determined in the fourth step, over the span of your virtual career path as follows:

Step five: Determine your career path		
Year	**Age**	**Planned action**
2009 - 2010	18 - 19 year	▪ CCNA (Cisco Certified Network Associate).
2010 - 2016	19 – 25 year	▪ Work in the IT field to gain varied IT experience.

Step five: Determine your career path (*continued*)		
Year	**Age**	**Planned action**
2010 - 2014	19-23 years	• Study a bachelor's degree in IT.
2014 - 2016	23 - 25 year	• Work in an IT-related position (preferably in another company), but at managerial level. • Study to acquire a professional qualification in Project Management (such as the American PMP) or MBA in IT.
2016 - ?	25-? years	• You are now qualified to achieve your career goal to work as "IT manager in a large company", either in your current firm or another one

Let's put these results into chart form:

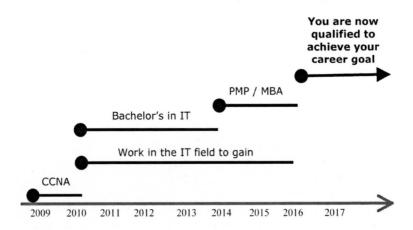

4. Career Planning at a Later Age

We will assume in this example that you are one of the those people who did not plan their career path at the beginning of their lives and bad luck was your nemesis, which has resulted in you being in the positioned we mentioned at the beginning of this book: "professional deadlock", "limited demand" or "end of the career life cycle" and you did not realize this until you reached your late forties!

Now, you perceive that time is very late for you to catch up and your working life is doomed to fail or stagnate and you develop a heightened degree of frustration!

But wait, you still can, with a little effort and with a little bit of concentration and proper planning, change the flow of your life in a way you would not dream of!

To demonstrate this, let us see how we can apply the methodology to help you out of your dilemma.

4.1. Step one: Determine your career goal

After identifying and becoming familiar with your internal constraints and studying the job market, let's suppose you decide that your career goal is to become "Head of Human Resources for a major company".

4.2. Step two: Determine required competencies for achieving your career goal

To be able to achieve your career goal, you must possess a set of professional and management skills that we can summarize as follows:

• **Educational and professional qualifications:**

- From an academic perspective:

You need to have a bachelor's degree, preferably in Human Resources in particular and in management in general.

- From a professional perspective:

It is the case that in the job market there is a high demand for people holding "Certified in Personnel Development" (CIPD) designation.

- From a management perspective:

Either a MBA qualification or CMI Executive Diploma in Strategic Management and Leadership (EDSML).

• **The necessary professional and managerial experience**

As we mentioned earlier, it is hard to place specific numbers relating to the years and types of experience necessary as this issue is largely relative and relies heavily on an individual's abilities, how focused they are, their interests and motivation.

In general terms, we can say the required expertise to achieve this career goal is twelve years: five years in the Human Resources field whereby almost three years are performed as a manager in Human Resources.

▪ Skills and talents:

Let us assume that in our case the most important skills are: ability to lead, ability to make decision, verbal and written communication skills, positive thinking, emotional intelligence, the art of listening, analysis skills and other skills that will be defined later based on nature of work.

To be able to understand this data more effectively, I suggest we put it in a table as follows:

Step two: Determine required competencies for achieving your career goal	
Qualifications	**Academic:** B.A, preferably in Human Resources **Professional:** Certified in Personnel Development (CIPD) **Management:** MBA or CMI Executive Diploma in Strategic Management and Leadership (EDSML).
Expertise	12 years, with 5 years in the field of Human Resources of which about 3 years are as a manager of Human Resources.
Skills	Ability to lead/ ability to make decision/ verbal and written communication/ positive thinking/ emotional intelligence/ the art of listening/ analysis skills and other skills that will be defined later.

4.3. Step three: Analyze your existing competencies

Let's suppose that, when trying to identify which of the competencies you possess, you find that you have those listed below:

Step three: Analyze your existing competencies	
Qualifications	**Academic:** B.A in Science – Physics **Professional:** not applicable **Management:** not applicable
Expertise	Varied 18 years in the public sector
Skills	**Strengths:** talking and listening, emotional intelligence, problems solving and writing. **Weakness:** the way you assess and look at things in general and to Human Resources in particular based on expertise in the public sector, which is different than that of the private sector.

4.4. Step four: Determine requirements to fill gaps
between what you actually possess of competencies and what is required for your career goal.

When comparing the two tables in Step two and Step three, we can determine them as follows in the following table:

Qualifications	**Academic:** nothing **Professional:** Certified in Personnel Development (CIPD) **Management:** MBA or CMI Executive Diploma in Strategic Management and Leadership (EDSML).
Expertise	5 years in the field of Human resources, three years of which are as a manager of human Resources
Skills	You have to develop your "understanding of the private sector" and other skills such as understanding and empathizing with others, ability to make decisions, leadership and others factors that will be defined later based on nature of work. For now you have to care about improving your skills and strive to pass the evaluation interviews so that you can move from the public sector into the profession, which you are targeting.

- **Competitive advantage "your key to the solution":**

In this table, we have determined what you have to possess to be able to become Head of Human Resources for a major company, but the question is where and how to begin?

You have to move into the human resources field, and it is highly recommended to be in the private sector! However the question is: what advantages do you have to make a firm in the private sector hire you in the human resources field, with a salary no less than your current salary, or even more?

The answer to this question is in your possessing "the key" that will open the door to the job market in the field of human resources to you. This key in our example is the highly accepted CIPD (Certified in Personnel Development) qualification.

So, the answer to our question, "how to begin", first you have to target the CIPD qualification as your passing, at least, of some of its units should enable you to move to the human resources field in the private sector.

4.5. Step five: Determine your career path that allows you to fill the gaps and arrive at your career goal.

Based on the fourth step, we can determine your career improvement path and define the necessary requirements to fill the gaps over the span of your virtual career path as follows:

Year	Age	Procedure to be planned
2009 – 2011	45 – 47 years	▪ Study the CIPD (Certified in Personnel Development) qualification. ▪ Improve your skills to pass the evaluation interviews.
2010 – 2012	46 – 48 years	▪ Move into a human resources role, maybe at first line management level, in the same organization you work for or in another organization.
2012 – 2015	48 – 51 years	▪ Move to an executive management level position in human resources, even in another organization. ▪ Study MBA or CMI Executive Diploma in Strategic Management and Leadership (EDSML)

2015 - ????	51 - ??? years	<ul><li>You are now qualified to achieve your career goal "Head of Human Resources" in a major company, either in the organization you work for, or in another organization.</li></ul>

Let's put these results into chart form:

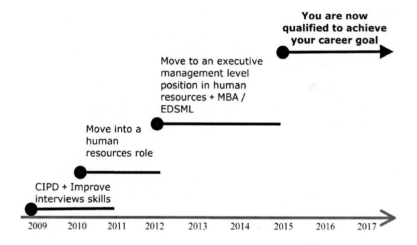

Summary:

In this book we have engaged in a discussion with regard to all of the tools and concepts required to plan your career path, followed by a discussion of four general models to help get you progress in planning your career path. Now it is up to you to begin planning your actual career path.

Based on my experience, each individual represents a unique model with unique talents and ambitions. You must therefore begin determining your career goal in order to map out your career path and plan the framework and details of your life.

I know it isn't easy, but it is even harder to let your life slip through your fingers. To make it easier, seek the help of those with specialized experience and gather the necessary information and data found on the Internet and in professional chartered bodies and other sources.

For any of you who would like to contact me, share your experience or knowledge with me, or comment on the book, please contact me by email at: **cdp@imc-middleeast.com**.